# Seventh Floor

Sonia Nouri

I dedicate this to the great spirit of my dear father. I believe you have become a separate source of energy, having detached yourself from your layers.

**Title**: Seventh Floor
**Author**: Sonia Nouri
**Translator**: Parsa Falsafi
**Paint**: Shahab Jafan Nejad
**ISBN**: 9781942912996
**Publisher**: Supreme Art, USA

*This book is not a story;*

*It's simply a formula for life*

**I dedicate this book to my dear Sonia
and congratulate myself on my birthday.**

April 22, 1993

# Introduction

Have we really been born just to struggle from morning till night for a little bit of happiness?

I don't think life is that superficial—or at least, our Creator, or whatever cause brought us and this world into existence, was not so simple as to make us engage in meaningless efforts. Surely, there is a dharma (our mission in this world) behind our birth, one that is more purposeful and well-planned than merely working hard to taste a drop of happiness. I was born to achieve my goals, to become complete, and to experience life—not just to survive.

If you look around, you will see that although objects, people, and places surround us, there are also invisible frequencies around us, storing specific information. Like radio waves, mobile signals, and more. But just because you can't see them doesn't mean they don't exist. All you have to do is turn on the radio and adjust the frequency slightly to find your favorite program.

With simple exercises, we want to learn how to control our thoughts and emotions. Thoughts are biochemical reactions in the brain that trigger the release of chemical signals. These chemical signals create the same feelings in your body that you had previously thought about. These emotions then generate new thoughts, which in turn produce more emotions. This cycle continues endlessly, and we want to take control of it.

To attain true awareness, you must let go of the past and the familiar things in your life, and instead focus on the unknown. It is only then that you create new possibilities, experiences, and emotions, and the mundane, repetitive aspects of life will lose their meaning.

I am not a philosopher with bizarre theories, nor a scientist with extraordinary discoveries. I am simply a human, just like those who read this book, with everyday failures. In a few chapters, I have summarized the lessons I have learned from my failures, or more accurately, I have shared a clearer perspective on life. This book is for those who seek change and want to become the person who remains truly significant.

When I realized that so many of us are unaware of our true selves, that we have forgotten our inner worth, and that we chase after empty, fleeting things, my heart was shaken. I felt a strong urge to tell everyone that who you truly are is far more valuable than doing anything merely to exist, to be noticed, to attract attention, or to spend a fortune on clothes just to look beautiful. I want to tell everyone that it's enough to just be a little more human. Humanity is timeless. It's time to captivate with your inner self and your mind, not just your appearance. I want to share peace with you, so you can make better decisions; because decision means choice, choice means path, and path means life. It's your desire to decide whether you want to be a person or just a little human!

One day, I had a dream while sleeping. It was so beautiful that I wished to see it again. I tried so hard to relive that dream, but I couldn't... So, I decided to make that dream come true.

**"I don't understand the light blue color of the walls. I think it should be a dark red, or perhaps..."**

The room is filled with bookshelves that stretch as far as the eye can see. Everything is in the most chaotic yet strangely organized way; the typewriter on the desk, tucked in the corner of the room, is at rest. The typewriter has thrown papers around, and a short man with a protruding belly, his hair frosted with age, picks up papers from the floor, the desk, and the surrounding shelves, stacking them one on top of the other. Each time he seems to lose an important paper; he looks around with irritation and arranges the papers as if solving a puzzle. The man, in his rumpled suit, looks as though he missed the school bus and, in a hurry, leaves the room. With folders full of papers sticking out from between the files, as if they want to move ahead of the man, but have become trapped between his chest and hands. The man quickens his pace to leave the house. Standing in front of the door, he looks up and down the building, then, calmly but with difficulty, presses the elevator button and impatiently waits for it to arrive. He mutters something to himself. He enters the elevator. When he exits the building and steps into the hustle and bustle of the city, we lose track of the man's words. The elderly man seems almost blind—he doesn't look around, nor does he let the noise of the city distract him. Like an arrow shot from its bow, he hurries toward his destination. Along the way, he bumps into people blocking his path, muttering under his breath as he passes by. He reaches a hospital at the edge of the city, stops, looks at the hospital, and straightens the papers hanging out of his hands. He takes a deep breath and boldly continues on his way. Just before reaching the hospital, a smile appears on his face, and he enters the building.

The walls of the hospital, painted in sky blue, seem to cover the artificial calmness that masks the stress of the people who have been hospitalized or passed away there. Some people are sitting on chairs, anxiously glancing around. Some are standing by the phones, searching for money to borrow. Others lie on the floor, mourning the loss of their loved ones with the most heartrending symphony in the world. I also see some people quietly leaning against the small window near the reception desk, insisting on being admitted until their money is ready. I just don't understand the light blue color of the walls. I think it should be a dark red, or perhaps....

The man, with his gaze fixed on the crowd, walks briskly. With his kind and pleasant face, he sends a message of help to the people, making his way as quickly as possible to the information booth.

A young man, dressed in guard-like clothes, sits on a chair inside a glass booth, guiding people with impatience and a slightly irritated tone. The man approaches the young man. So absorbed in his conversation with others, the young man doesn't notice his presence. The man taps on the glass two or three times.

Man: *I want to see the hospital director... sir.*

He knocks harder on the glass, and the young man looks at him angrily.

Man: *I want to see the hospital director.*

Young man: *(in an angry, sarcastic tone) Not possible, sir!*

The man, as if he hadn't heard the young man's response, repeats himself.

Man: I want to see the hospital director.

The young man, now irritated, stands up and approaches the man.

Young man: *Do you hear what I'm saying? It's not possible! There's no director here at all.*

The man repeats his request again.

Man: *I want to see the hospital director.*

The young man mutters under his breath, grabs his phone, and dials a number.

Young man: *Sir, there's a madman here disturbing the peace. Come and deal with him.*

The man, stressed yet oddly pleased, pushes his glasses closer to his eyes, with the items in his hands forcing the action. His round face becomes visible, his flushed cheeks peeking through the gray beard. Two large men, with massive frames, long beards, and ridiculous things in their ears that seem to have strangled themselves in their wires, approach the man.

One of them says: *Sir, please step outside.*

The man gives them a once-over, looking them up and down.

Man: *I want to see the hospital director.*

Ignoring the man's words, they grab his hands.

The man frees his hand, steps back slightly, and says more loudly:

*I want to save the people. Where is the hospital director?*

The word *save* was so soothing to the crowd that a silence took over the room, and only the deep voice of the middle-aged man could be heard.

*This hospital has no director! I'm Doctor, Joseph, George, William, Ali... whatever you like to call me.*

He approaches the towering men, whose beard sizes have weighed heavily on their reason and dragged their minds downward. Despite trying to look angry, his radiant face refuses to appear anything but pleasant.

*I want to see the hospital director.*

It was at that moment that I, the youngest doctor in the hospital, arrived. These kinds of arguments happened every day, which was a lie; but every other day, they would occur in the hospital, and I would pass by indifferent, as most of the insults were directed at me.

The hospital director never kept his promises, and he didn't manage certain affairs properly. The curses and insults were always directed at me, but this time, for the first time, I wanted to stop and understand the reason. As I got closer to the commotion, I made my way through the crowd toward the middle-aged man. The towering figures, whom I called the brainless giants, stepped aside when they saw me.

"Hello, Doctor," I cleared my throat.

*What's the matter?*

*This man has been here since morning, saying he wants to see the hospital director, that he wants to save the people, and all this nonsense!*

*Since when did saving people become nonsense?*

The man didn't look at me, and with a sadness as though his ships had sunk, he seemed upset with me.

I moved closer to him.

*I'm the hospital's psychologist. Is there anything I can help you with?*

The man turned and looked at me, a look that even now, when I remember it, brings a smile to my lips.

The man spoke quietly, like a child not wanting anyone to hear him:

*How many words can we speak together?*

Despite hearing the usual whispers of men and women who, because of my appearance and my work situation, envied me, I ignored them and moved closer to the man. I then took him upstairs to my office. Women with strange, artificial or plastic faces, drowned in makeup that reflected their empty thoughts, with long nails like demons and exaggerated protrusions that seemed like something from a Dadaist caricature. In another corner, there were whispers of women whose ugly thoughts were hidden beneath sheets. They mocked me under their breath, saying things like: *'What an indecent woman, she's crazy, how lucky she is...'*, and so on.

And in contrast to them, there were men, full of lusts that reeked, who, in order to have a word with the seductive women, would endorse them.

I never allowed myself to respond to them because I didn't speak their language. I believed that if I stopped for even a second to say something, years would pass, and I would be left only facing this heap of nonsense. I would just smile at them, a smile that if they knew the meaning of, they'd realize they needed to correct themselves. Women with strange, artificial or plastic faces, covered in makeup reflecting their shallow thoughts, long nails like demons, and exaggerated features that belonged more in a Dadaist cartoon. In another corner, there were whispers from women whose ugly thoughts were hidden under their sheets. They mocked me quietly, saying things like, 'What an indecent woman, she's crazy, how lucky she is...'.

Meanwhile, there were men, filled with lust that reeked, who, just to get a word in with the seductive women, would praise them.

I never allowed myself to respond to them, because I didn't speak their language. I thought that if I stopped even for a moment to reply, years would pass, and all I'd be left with would be this pile of nonsense. Instead, I'd just smile at them—a smile that, if they knew its meaning, would have shown them that they should correct themselves.

We stood in front of the elevator, and I was constantly worried that the man might run away! My eyes were fixed on him, almost trapping him with my gaze. Then, the elevator arrived in front of us. I grabbed his hand, and like a calm child, he followed me. We entered the elevator and stood facing the crowd in the lobby. As the elevator doors closed, the noise, the hustle, and the commotion came to an end. A soothing melody began to play from the elevator's speakers, and my heartbeat slowed. The man's anxious and troubled face slowly disappeared, replaced by one filled with calmness. The elevator stopped on the seventh floor. The doors opened, and we both stepped into the hallway. It was a long corridor, devoid of any furnishings or objects! It seemed like no one had ever entered here before, yet everything was neat, calm, and perfectly in its place. I could sense his confusion and bewilderment from the look in his eyes. When we reached the end of the hallway, we stood in front of my office door. The man struggled, shifting the files in his hands up and down. I searched for the key to my office, shaking my bag to find it. I was so agitated and nervous that, suddenly, I saw the man quietly open the door to my office; as if he had never needed a key in the first place!

It was a large room, filled with items, books, and scattered papers that were left abandoned on the floor and desk. Crumpled pieces of paper, like snowballs, were thrown around the room. Broken-framed photos and indistinct images were nailed to the walls. The man looked at my disorganized room, which had no place to sit, and secretly observed me. It felt like it was the first time I had seen my own room. Nothing was in its place! To be honest, I had never allowed anyone into my room before, except for myself. My meeting room and workspace were three floors down, and every day a maid cleaned and tidied that area. I don't know why I pressed the button for the seventh floor in the elevator. Of course, I knew exactly where everything was, but still, I always spent a lot of time looking for it. The old man gave me a glance with a smile, probably sensing my embarrassment through my eyes, and tried to reassure me with his own smile. He moved closer to my bookshelf, and I was utterly embarrassed! With a mixture of surprise and a smile, he seemed puzzled as to how a faceless photo frame could end up among pedagogical storybooks, articles about meaningless people dressed in crumpled clothes, and wedged between all those scripts of fluoxetine, sertraline, and books on love and hate. I cleared my throat, hid my embarrassment behind my face, and tidied up the couch to make space for the man. The room was so cluttered with things that, in that moment, I couldn't figure out which ones were useful. Distracted, I kept moving my belongings from one side to the other. The man placed the files he was holding in a corner and made his way toward a wooden chair by the window. On it, I had placed a box full of memories from my past. It had been months, maybe years, since I organized them and put them in the box to take to storage—but I kept forgetting! To be honest, sometimes, when I had nothing else to do, I would open it and spend hours sifting through those memories. The man seemed to know exactly what was inside that box.

He struggled to lift the heavy box and, like something foul-smelling and leaking, carried it to the door and placed it outside. He slammed the door shut and exhaled deeply. I stood still, torn between feeling upset at how he had discarded my box of memories and relieved that there was now space to sit. I motioned toward the chair for the old man to sit and begin.

*How can I help you?*

The old man, with his gentle face and the deep lines that traced his life story, gave me a smile that was both wise and a little sad.

*I want to save people.*

*And who are you to make such a claim?*

*It doesn't matter who I am. What matters is that I've come at a time to heal, to help those who are lost. A time when people don't know what to do with their lives, when they've become prisoners of their routines and repetition.* The other children no longer have dreams, they have all lost their hope, love no longer exists, and humanity has disappeared.

The disease that exists among all of you is more dangerous than you can imagine, and delaying its treatment even for a moment is not an option. The cure is that all of you must contract the illness that I have!

The man kept speaking these strange and bizarre words. I was scared, but there was a sense of trust in him that brought me comfort, and I wanted to listen to him to see where this was going. I maintained my composure, making sure not to be disrespectful, and I said:

May I ask what your illness is?

An illness that we can call anything. It's just that everyone must be infected with it. This is the health that the general public needs, and it's a truth that they've been unaware of for years. And anyone who knows the truth has kept it hidden for themselves; but I, in order for everyone to taste the sweetness of true life, must make everyone infected with it.

I didn't understand a word of what the man was saying, and I conveyed this to him with my wide eyes, which seemed to be popping out of my face, just looking at him.

The old man, as if he were about to start a long discussion, took a deep breath, took off his coat, and laid it on the back of the chair. He leaned his upper body against his knees, tilted toward me, and with his eyes full of hope, began to speak.

With complete calmness, and drawing from the things I had learned in books and my counseling sessions, I created a peaceful environment to allow him to speak about his illness without stress or fear.

# Chapter one

## I love myself

One day, just like any other day, I woke up in a messy room where the broken window didn't let go of the cold draft. Torn curtains hung from the ceiling to the floor, decorating the room, while the blazing sunlight poured into my eyes. The sound of the plastic sheet I had placed over the broken window echoed, as I foolishly thought it would block the wind, but instead, the wind just brought more noise into the room. The murmurs of people who didn't know what they were doing filled the room with confusion. I struggled to open my eyes and had no desire to leave my bed. Instead of feeling grateful that another day had been added to my life, I woke up with a heavy heart, thinking, *"Damn... how am I supposed to make it through this day and turn it into night?"*

Back then, getting through the day felt like the hardest thing imaginable. I'd lost my job, and regret was the only thing I had left.

Trapped in my own mess, I had grown dependent— emotionally entangled with someone who, ironically, had already left me too.

To pass the time, I numbed my lungs with cigarettes and poisoned my liver with alcohol—just to keep the chaos and panic at bay, just to make it to night.

I had wrapped myself so tightly in my blanket that even if I tried to get up, the blanket seemed unwilling to let me go.

But eventually, to silence the growl of my empty stomach, I dragged myself out of that cocoon of fabric I'd buried myself in. I sat at the edge of the bed for a few seconds, hunched over so badly it was as if I had been denied the blessing of a spine—like I'd lived a life without one.

All I wanted was to throw myself back onto the bed and continue drowning in my daydreams.

But an empty stomach doesn't care about dreams.

In that moment, survival was the only option.

Like some kind of crawling creature, I dragged myself forward on my knees, inching closer to the kitchen.

A kitchen that was messy and filthy, with scraps of food scattered in every corner, and the constant buzz of flies announcing their presence over the leftovers. With nowhere clean to sit or eat, and not a shred of motivation to clean up the mess around me, I threw on whatever clothes I could find to go out and grab some breakfast.

The clothes had been tossed onto the couch weeks ago, balled up in such a way that it was as if I'd planned ahead—knowing I wouldn't have the energy to look for anything else.

And so, I stepped out.

Our home was part of a massive residential complex. Spiral staircases formed the spine of the building, and the elevator—well, it had been "almost ready" since the very first day I moved in.

Seven years later, and it's still under maintenance.

I lived on the seventh floor, near the rooftop.

Going up and down those stairs was pure torment.

Every time I looked down through the metal railings that encircled the stairwell, I'd let out a sigh soaked in hopelessness.

Muttering curses under my breath, I stomped my feet on each step as if I was taking revenge on the lifeless stairs themselves. As I passed each floor or unit, I couldn't help but notice how poorly the building had been constructed, as if it had been made of straw. From each apartment, not the sound of life, but the sound of mere survival leaked out of the neighbors' hollow bodies.

Some of those sounds were like my own memories, others like my worries, and sometimes they were the fears that haunted me.

Because of this, I'd always feel more exhausted by the time I reached the ground floor.

If I could somehow make it through that, I'd step out onto the street, and that's when the real challenge began.

Our building was in the middle of the city. From the rich to the middle class, and from the poor to the destitute, people wandered there—every kind of human being, along with animals, were clearly visible.

The blaring horns of cars would rip through your sleep.

The sounds of arguments and brawls would distract you.

The street vendors advertising their goods were laughable—how many sweet lies they had woven into their daily sales pitches. Lies like, *"This is the last one! The sale is over!"*

Meanwhile, they had an entire storage unit of those very items... *"The ones you ordered are in!"*

Though I knew everything they said was a lie, it wasn't painful. It was just funny. I sat at the table, waiting for my breakfast to be prepared, forced to stare out of the window. What I saw was an odd scene. People brushed past each other angrily, moving without any sense of direction, unaware of where they were heading.

The strangest figure in this chaotic crowd was a mother—her baby on her back, extending a hand in front of people, begging, following them for a few steps, repeating the same action with relentless persistence, without showing any signs of fatigue.

Some people ignored her and continued on their way. Others stopped, pressing a crumpled coin or bill into her hand.

After begging a few people, she counted the money in her hand, gently set the child down on the curb, ran a hand over her disheveled hair, and with a face flushed red from the slaps of begging she tried to hide, but couldn't, entered the café where I was sitting.

Without meaning to, my gaze followed her. It was as if I wanted to know the end of her story.

She entered the café, walked up to the counter, and carefully unfolded the crumpled bills she had been holding. Even though they were still bent, she placed them on the counter.

-*"Two hot bread rolls, please."*

The man behind the counter took the crumpled bills, counted them, and his condescending glance from top to bottom irritated me. With a sense of superiority, he placed the bread rolls on the table, and the woman eagerly picked them up.

As the man was about to give her the change, she graciously handed it back to him, then fluttered like a little sparrow toward her child.

The child, overjoyed, hugged his mother, and they both sat on the curb, eating with such enjoyment, as if they were eating a steak with special sauce. They must have felt this was their only joy in life.

At that moment, my breakfast was brought to me. I glanced at the meal I always ordered, but it wasn't the same as usual. I felt as if maybe this tray could offer me a moment of happiness too.

I began to eat, but unlike that woman, I couldn't find joy in it. I had no purpose but to pass the time.

It was a strange day. Perhaps today was the day I had been seeking the courage for all along—the day of farewell to life... the day of farewell to life. After finishing my breakfast, I stood up and saw myself in the café's window. It felt as though I hadn't looked into a mirror for years. I liked my face, but alas, I knew I would never see it again.

I was so engrossed in gazing at myself in the glass and smiling at myself that I didn't notice a young man standing on the other side of the window. He must have thought I saw him because he waved at me and laughed.

Embarrassed, I quickly turned away and left the café.

On the street, I quickened my pace. As usual, I had to send an email to my former lover who had left me.

When I was on my way back home, I searched for the book vendor, but to my surprise, I didn't see him. Instead, an old mysterious man, a cigarette vendor, was sitting there.

This man held a strange symbol for me. His face, full of longing and without a word, brought death closer to people. He sold cigarettes, which, for him, seemed worth the price of death's proximity. I walked up to him and took a cigarette, ready to end my life.

I entered the building, stopped at the stairs, and looked up at the stairs leading to my apartment. I wanted to sigh when our neighbor saw me.

-*"Hello! You've gained so much weight! I guess all that work has kept you away from exercise, or maybe life has just caught up with you."*

Without thinking, I looked down at my protruding stomach. Under my breath, I cursed the neighbor, irritated by his audacity, and wondered if he had no life of his own that he'd be thinking about my fat or my wasted muscles. I controlled myself and just smiled.

I climbed the stairs, but this time not because I wanted to reach my home, but simply to get away from the woman's gaze.

My breath was short, and sweat covered my face. It seemed the neighbor's rude comment was right; I had indeed gained weight.

When I got home, I rushed to the faucet. Water came down slowly, as if it were making me work for it, and I had to beg it to give me even a little sip.

Afterward, I went to the mirror. I looked at myself and my body—how covered in dust I was, just like the things in my house, buried beneath a layer of neglect.

The days, or maybe the hours, that I had lost count of had passed by while I had been unaware of myself.

Out of habit, I went to my laptop to check my email. I looked at the inbox—no new messages, as usual.

Angrily, I closed the laptop and rested my head on the desk, leaning on my arm.

I wanted to end this life. I stood up, grabbed the pills I had taken months ago, and prepared to swallow them. But before doing so, I wanted to send an email to that heartless person. I wanted her to know that when my body was found, and the stench of decay filled the building, it wouldn't be because of her.

Perhaps after my death, her conscience would hurt. Though, if she had a conscience, she wouldn't have treated me this way.

In an instant, as if something was guiding me, I opened the laptop and started writing the letter to myself.

*... My dear, I miss you.*

I pulled back a little and looked at the screen of my laptop in surprise, then I wrote again.

*Today, after such a long time, I saw you by accident in a café. How broken you looked. All the strength you once had is gone. It's all my fault that I forgot you. I was the one who ignored you, and now look how weak you've become.*

*Tears were streaming down my face. I had gone mad, but I was writing a letter to myself, pressing down on the keyboard with whatever thoughts came to my mind.*

*In my eyes, you were the strongest person I'd ever seen. You've dealt with all these problems. See how much I love you, how much I long for your scent. I miss the warmth of your embrace. You are my only possession, the only one who completes me when we are together. Please forgive me. You were the one who saved me in the worst conditions. My dear, we survived those days and nights. Now, with a breeze, we can't fall apart. When the storm came, instead of turning to you, I turned to someone I didn't even know. They lost me. Find me... I am yours. You, the kind and loving one, must rise. You should not sit still. You are the wise one, the mature one. Without you, I am nothing. Forgive me... For the beauty of your existence, the clarity of your heart. you are within me. I am asking you to guide me so that I may find my way...*

I was so absorbed in writing that time slipped away from me. Sometimes I cried, and sometimes I laughed. The pills in my hand had fallen onto the keyboard and got stuck between the keys; it seemed like my laptop had taken my hands and emptied my fist, and instead of the pills, it held my hands in its grip. When I lifted my head, I realized it was getting dark, and I had written nearly seventy pages of a letter to myself. It's ridiculous, isn't it? No! It's the most amazing feeling in the world; I knew all the words and had memorized all the beautiful sentences, but I was spending them for someone else—someone I didn't even know if would read or understand. Maybe it's better to say I was wasting them. For the first time, I was upset that it was bedtime. I wanted to take a shower and wear the clothes I had bought months ago, the ones I had planned to wear for him when he came, but now, I wanted to wear them for myself and invite myself to dinner. I wanted to listen to the best music and laugh loudly, but time passed so quickly, and it was too late. I was afraid to sleep! What if there was no morning, and I wouldn't be able to do all these things? I felt like someone who had just made up with someone she hadn't spoken to in years, with so many unsaid words. The self I had lost all those years ago with her arrival. I realized that everything I had wanted from her was the same as what I wanted from myself.

With these thoughts, I fell asleep on the couch, like a child who had been invited to her favorite party but had fallen asleep. When I woke up in the morning, I jumped out of bed, looked around, and unconsciously, a word came to my lips:

Thank God

I wouldn't say I was unfamiliar with this word; but I definitely hadn't used it in a long time. I quickly went towards the bathroom.

When I came back from the bathroom, I could smell the pleasant scent of shampoo, soap, and... I always felt sad after a shower thinking about who would dry all this hair, what clothes to wear... I put on some clothes and decided to clean the house; but before that,

I wanted to write letters to myself again and praise myself. I started writing:

*My dear, good morning*

I want to pamper you and have breakfast peacefully together. I woke up early today to see you again. Thank God! I want you to know that these days, when you wake up every morning, it's not without reason. You must fulfill the responsibility you were born with, complete your mission, or else, if your mission had been finished, you wouldn't have woken up today, just like the man from the downstairs apartment.

I didn't know what I was writing, I was scared of my own words. I heard shouting and screaming from outside. Maybe I was hearing it, but I was lost in writing. I quickly went to the door, opened it, and I could hear the cries and shouts of my neighbor more clearly. Secretly, so no one would see me, I looked down from the top of the stairs; the woman was jumping up and down like a spark. With a stretcher, an ambulance was taking a body out of the house. I was scared, I quickly went inside and closed the door. I sat in silence for a few seconds, unable to think of anything. How did I write such words to myself? Maybe someone is really talking to me, maybe I've gone crazy. Whatever it was, in that moment, I couldn't go to my laptop.

I started tidying up the house, but my mind kept wandering back to the letters I had written to myself. Every little thing I put in its place and cleaned gave me a sense of success. It was so strange! I had always avoided cleaning the house, but now I was doing it with enthusiasm, setting little goals for myself to tidy up. Nothing had changed except for me. The same sounds came from outside, the same moments that I would have given my life to escape from, but now it felt like a new person was beside me, and I enjoyed spending time with them. It was getting close to sunset, and the house was neat and clean. A warm soup was cooking on the stove. I looked at my house from afar. How lovely it was! A smile unconsciously appeared on my lips. I made myself some tea, went to my laptop, and continued my unfinished letter.

Darling, thank you for everything you've done. Thank you for cleaning our home with your beautiful hands, so we could sit and drink tea together while waiting for dinner to be ready. You must be tired!

It might sound silly, but it's the best exercise to begin your story.

Writing letters to myself became my daily ritual—every hour of every day. I used to write everything I had to my ex-love, empowering him, making him strong and ruthless. But then I started writing to myself, and I realized how much every person needs to hear these words. And when they come from yourself, their impact is even deeper—because you know they're from the heart, with no tricks, no ulterior motives. Just a pure desire to lift yourself higher and grow more successful every day. That's the essence of true love (we'll explore this more in the next chapters). Who knows you more truly than yourself? And who is more eagerly waiting for your success than you are? I knew that every word I wrote would, sooner or later, become reality. Because I had lived through the fears of my past, I knew that if I gave voice to my dreams and my moments of joy, I would live those too. The more letters I wrote to myself, the more I fell in love with myself—day by day.

One beautiful morning, I woke up and, as usual, began writing a letter to myself. That's when I received an email from him. I had no desire to open it. I realized then that the only thing that had made him seem so big in my life were the words I had once given him. And now, because I hadn't directed any of those words toward him in the past week, he had grown small—

and was now the one searching for me. Without opening the email, I deleted it. And I continued loving myself.

P.S. (A nod to *Sophie's World*)

To begin, the first nudge must come from within—you need to call out to yourself, make peace with yourself, or better yet, find yourself. To make peace, you have to humble yourself before your own heart. And to do that, you must choose the most beautiful words. Now that you've made peace with yourself, spend a few days falling in love with you.

Postscript to the Postscript:

Words carry immense power—we know this deep down, we just don't fully believe it. If I call myself a fool for seven days straight, by the seventh day, I'll become the greatest fool in the world. Now imagine I change that word, and for seven days, I use the most beautiful compliments and traits to describe myself. Even if I haven't fully become those qualities by the seventh day, at the very least, I'll have come to believe in them—and with time, I'll begin to live them. It's like when you're at a gathering and someone tells you, *'You speak so eloquently,'* and you like the sound of it. For the rest of the event, you'll try to speak more eloquently—and in doing so, you'll experience it. And if you stay at that gathering for seven days, that eloquence might just become a lasting part of you. Now, write down the best quality you see in yourself—because when you want to preserve a trait, you begin to honor it. Daily practice becomes a habit, and a habit becomes your way of life. Starting today, call yourself by your best qualities: the strongest, the smartest, the most eloquent—whatever it is you wish to become, call yourself that. This is how you make peace with yourself. And by doing this, you hold on to the energy you've instilled in yourself and begin your life with renewed energy. These simple exercises have a profound impact.

To work out hard, you first warm up to get ready.

(In other words) Making peace with my inner self.

Many of us have forgotten ourselves due to the hard circumstances of life. We lost track of our energy and spent it on others instead of investing it in ourselves.

I firmly say this is wrong, and this energy is hollow and ineffective. That's why we won't receive appropriate responses from it.

Energy becomes more powerful when it comes from the source. Where is your source of energy? Inside yourself.

Because, like you, I too had forgotten this source, and every day its energy diminished (sometimes it even went out completely).

The hollow, weak energy that came without a source couldn't help me focus or achieve what I wanted. In the end, only exhaustion, failure, despair, and hopelessness came to me. And foolishly, I was left searching for answers to my questions:

Why is a good response bad?

Why is no one like me?

Why can't I finish my things?

In those moments, I was asking myself the kind of questions that made death feel like the only answer. The first time I called out to myself—whether written on paper or spoken softly in front of a mirror or however I felt most comfortable, the first thing happened to me, was my eyes filled with tears. It was as if I had been punishing my own innocent inner child, denying her even the sound of her own name. In that moment, I felt both ashamed and deeply compassionate. I wanted to embrace myself, to listen patiently to the sobbing within, and to soothe it with love. and just by calling out to myself, I felt a surge of energy—like a spark had lit the long-forgotten source inside me, ignited by the sound of my own cries. now

I spoke a kind word about myself, and unconscious smile appeared on my lips. It felt as if the pure, innocent love of my childhood had reached out to me. (I truly encourage you: do these exercises with me.) To begin rebuilding trust in myself, I started to apologize—without shame—for all the times I had neglected, silenced, or abandoned myself; It was the sweetest apology I had ever made. at first, my inner self resisted—as if she had just realized the depth of everything she had been denied. But I welcomed the resistance with patience. I pleaded with her lovingly, and wrote to her with the most beautiful words I could find. And honestly, it was extraordinary. Through my words, I promised: I will never leave you again. the energy source began to awaken. and in that moment, I became a powerful woman, with the strongest, most loyal support I could ever have; myself. I kept repeating this ritual every day, and over time, that inner source grew stronger, more vibrant. even though nothing had changed in my external world, I had changed. now I could move through each day, handling even the smallest tasks, with strength, presence, and peace. The only difference? A light had been turned on within me. And that light gave me the certainty that I could move forward, powerfully.

Everything in this world is energy; our soul, our actions, and our reactions.

Without the soul, the body is useless. And without the body, we have no way to act. So, everything comes back to the soul. It is energy that gives the body its function, if you charge this energy positively, you move forward with a higher frequency. But if you feed it negativity, the body begins to decay, leading to illness. energy drives the actions we take, and the results of those actions shape our lives. (Think of Newton's law: *For every action, there is an equal and opposite reaction.*) If you act with negative energy, it's only natural that the reaction you'll face is also negative.

But if you act with positive energy, you receive *two* positive outcomes: first, you strengthen your inner source and second, you attract positive reactions to your actions. So, starting today, practice sending the best energy to yourself.

This energy powerfully influences your mind. Your mind shapes your decisions, your decisions shape your choices, your choices shape your path and ultimately, your life. All great things are born from simple practices.

When you shift your focus away from objects, people, places, and time and instead turn your attention to the vastness of life, the universe, and your inner being; your brain begins to change. neural networks that had become disconnected due to lack of focus start reconnecting, creating a more integrated and harmonious state in your brain. and when the brain becomes more organized, you become more aligned and balanced. To summarize; when your brain functions better, you feel better. If you truly want to change, you must let go of lower emotions like; guilt, pain, fear, shame, emptiness, so that you can rise into higher, more elevated feelings.

**Simply put,**

A person becomes complete only when they reconnect with their inner self.

The outer self, on its own, can mislead you and cause you pain. when I was living only half of a life; disconnected from that inner "me"; my relationships kept falling apart in strange, painful ways. because I was seeking completeness but not in my self, instead, I begged others to give me what I was missing. and when I beg, I get cheap. I become smaller, weaker. soon, I was wandering through life with low self-confidence, trying to fill an inner emptiness with anything I could find. but the more I tried, the more I lost myself. I had become someone who constantly gave in; Not out of kindness, but out of need.

Not because I wanted to, but because I couldn't bear the emptiness inside me. I never truly filled that emptiness. I just stuffed it with the wrong things— distractions that looked like love or purpose, but weren't. It's like trying to fill a missing puzzle piece with a chunk of Lego. It doesn't fit. It never will. eventually, I understood; that empty space was mine. It existed because I had stopped seeing myself. and only I could fill it. to heal, I had to start calling out to the version of me I had silenced. to gently invite her back to where she belonged. but let's be honest; expecting her to return after one call is foolish.

she didn't disappear overnight. she faded away slowly, after being ignored again and again. and so, she needs to be seen again and again; with patience, with softness, without pause, and without giving up.

… Loving yourself is the most important thing you can do. everything becomes more beautiful after that. this kind of self-love isn't arrogance or narcissism;

It's simply respect and appreciation for who you are. love yourself the way you did as a child; innocently, wholeheartedly, and without condition. we were all born this way. a child is naturally joyful, naturally in love with themselves. they adore everything about themselves. they express emotions freely. when they're happy, everyone knows it. and when they're sad, they cry out without shame or hesitation. they live fully in the present; fearless and full of wonder. we were all born this way; with love, with courage, constantly in awe of ourselves. but over time; because of society, our environment, or the pressures around us; we forgot. we stopped leaving room for self-appreciation. reconnecting with ourselves, at any age, is essential. It's the simplest and most profound path to success. all it takes is;

giving a little time to yourself. eventually, you'll realize that the only time you truly lived…was the time you spent with yourself. If you dedicate just one hour out of the 24 to yourself (To reflect. To be silent. To admire who you are.) to just be, without doing anything, to wait. To learn. To be patient; by the end of that day, you'll be amazed. because you'll see that the other 23 hours were lived unconsciously. and now, with renewed energy and a clear mind, you'll seek out the best paths for your journey; because now, you believe in yourself.

# Chapter two

There must be a God; for a human to be able to carry on.

In those days, when I was truly enjoying every moment; living, speaking, even exercising; I found myself unconsciously repeating a single phrase:

*"Thank you, God..."*

It felt strange to me at first, but somehow, saying those words worked like magic. they made me look more closely at what I did have, and kept bringing that positive energy into my life every time I said them. but then I asked myself; who was I really thanking? God?

That feeling of gratitude had sparked a curiosity in me: where is God? Managing all these people; isn't that a hard job? All this beauty in nature surely isn't for nothing. What kind of being creates so many things; big, small, weak, powerful; and for what purpose? Who is my Creator? Is my God different from the God of someone with a disability? different from the God of trees, or dogs? As these questions were surrounding my mind, and the depth of them were blowing my head; I walked out of my room and looked around the house. I could feel a positive energy in the tidy space; a home where once there had been sobs, tears, sighs, and curses, but now was filled with the sound of self-praise. I truly believed I was the best. and the energy inside me felt so real, so strong, that it seemed to affect my surroundings, which reflected it back to me. (You must praise yourself with such certainty and belief that your frequency radiates outward and bounces back at you; but it has to be genuine.); Still, all of that didn't ease the chaos in my mind. The more I thought, the more questions overwhelmed me. I knew, deep down, that I came from something. I'd read different interpretations of it; that I came from a cluster of multiplying cells, from the instinct to survive, from energy, or from a soul. I wanted to find my origin; the thing that had designed me. but the deeper I went, the more my thoughts wandered down paths I couldn't control. It was as if my mind already knew things, things it had hidden from me; waiting for me to come looking. everything has a reason for existing. my brain and mind were urging me to discover their own existence. maybe God is our mind, our consciousness. but that answer didn't satisfy me. It felt more like an escape from a higher truth. so, I opened my laptop. after writing a few lines, I suddenly typed a question; Who is God?; followed by a long line of question marks. I kept thinking as I sketched diagrams on paper. If God is energy, then it's a powerful energy; one that's surrounded itself with a protective field, so nothing can harm it. and because it's so powerful, it's capable of anything. so it must be the source of all energy, able to emit its own force, feeding other sources of energy. and if I could get close to that energy; or act in ways that align with it; then maybe I could become a source of energy, too. but I couldn't accept that I came from a simple chain of cell replications; from non-living matter that somehow reacted and turned into me. That just didn't sit right. I couldn't believe that I was formed through chemical reactions or that evolution alone, for the sake of survival, explained it all. I couldn't fully trust my own reasoning; or disprove it either. my mind was growing more and more restless. But the further I went, the more I felt like the reason for my existence did exist; and it was the same thing, just called by different names. In every region, every climate, every country, people had translated it in their own way, based on their understanding. but at its core, they were all pointing to the same thing. I couldn't handle these strange; yet strangely sweet; thoughts anymore. I sat down on the couch in front of the TV, grabbed the remote, hoping maybe the television would take control of my mind and change the channel in my head. after flipping through several channels, I landed on an American film. It was showing clips of the movie and highlighting all the awards it had won. Wanting to distract myself from all those overwhelming questions, I decided to watch. It turned out to be a documentary about a famous director; someone who made films that won every major award and was hailed as the greatest director in history. People had so much faith in his work that sometimes they'd give him awards before even seeing the film. part of my mind was watching, while another part; the subconscious, filled with questions; started drawing parallels. I began placing my questions inside the framework of the movie, hoping a small metaphor might lead me to a deeper understanding. a thought came to me; maybe God is a director, and each of us is playing out a script He's written. I was sure He must be a master director; the challenging script of my life was proof enough. No amateur takes on a screenplay this difficult. at that moment, to me, He was nothing less than Hitchcock himself. now imagine; all these people in the world with their own difficult lives, and He's managing them all. that must mean He's incredibly powerful. then another thought hit me; if He's that skilled, then this must be the best script. Which means I have to play the best role in it. and that means; it's definitely not an easy one. but because it's a hard role, I realized; I'm the hero of this story. still, a little voice asked; what if the script itself is flawed? but no; He's the best director. I just have to believe in Him. even if the script in my hands is painfully difficult, if the director is strong, then I'm going to win the Oscar. you just have to trust the Director; just like an actor who receives a screenplay from Hitchcock. he doesn't question it, doesn't even read it before accepting. not because he knows the script is good, but because he trusts Hitchcock. that was my analysis in that moment; and I knew, without a doubt, that it was true. all I had to do was look out the window at the city; people walking, riding, lights flickering on and off in buildings. I could tell: each of them had their own story, and each was playing out their role, struggling in their own way. but why are the stories so different? It goes back to that simple analogy; every actor plays their role differently. Each of us has our own level of understanding, awareness, and intellect. And if we think, even just a little, we might be able to navigate the challenges we face. maybe it's our guides that misled us, that pulled us off course. But even for that, God gave us a powerful tool; reason. Through thinking, through awareness, we can recognize the pitfalls. With insight, we can see them. With willpower, we can survive them. each of us carries a set of gifts inside; maybe the story we've been given is written based on those very talents. realizing that my life story was written by God brought me peace. It made me understand that my failures weren't meaningless; they carried lessons. They were telling me that I either lacked the awareness to navigate the path, or I needed to fall; to wake up, to let go of the reason I fell, or even to change my direction. and when I succeeded, it meant I should study the path I'd taken; so, I could apply that same understanding to other areas of my life. So, in the end, I came up with a simple formula; One story, called Life. One actor, called Human. One assistant director, called Reason. all coming together under the direction of God; that is our creation. that was the analysis that came to me while watching the documentary. and I wanted to keep watching, just to find more pieces of the puzzle; to keep mapping them into my own story. The documentary continued with some of the criticism; mostly from uneducated people; aimed at the skilled director. but he never responded. He just smiled and walked away. maybe God is the same. when people criticize life, He simply smiles without replying; because He knows He's created a masterpiece that the critic lacks the depth to understand. a great director doesn't make films for the masses; he creates for those who get it. God has left the path to success and fulfillment open; but only those who understand will reach it. once again, I thought of the film's audience, which fell into three groups. The first group would praise the movie just because they knew the director was great; even if they didn't understand a thing. The second group didn't get it at all and dismissed it as ridiculous. But the third group; the ones who truly understood; they just sat back and enjoyed, soaking it in. for them, God has created a masterpiece; and He knows it. so, in front of those who don't understand, He doesn't need to say anything. He just smiles. In that moment, having made peace with myself, I realized I'd been part of the first group; the ones who said, 'Life is beautiful because I know God is great,' but hadn't really felt the depth of that truth. I'd placed myself in that group because I wanted to believe; because I knew God was the director of this world, so surely there must be something deep behind it, even if I didn't grasp it yet. but this realization stirred something in me. I wanted to become like those few rare people who *do* understand; the ones who truly feel it, and enjoy life on that deeper level. They were few, and no one ever crowded around them. but they had this quiet, undeniable peace about them. this is what I wanted. so, I had to put in the effort to walk the path that leads to understanding. there were times when the weight of my problems wore me down, when I felt drained. but the moment I reminded myself who the Director was, I felt hope rise again. I would move forward with more determination, and my energy would rise dramatically. so, the very first thing we need to understand is; that God must exist, in order for human beings to truly live. when you reach that awareness; that God is a great power, and that you can connect with Him, communicate with Him; everything changes. all it takes is one walk in nature. feel the scent of the earth. touch the bark of a tree. taste the warmth of the sunlight. watch the crashing waves as they strike like flashes of lightning. These are all parts of God. all of them are pieces of the source. when you come to that realization, you understand; God is everywhere.

## PS.

What is God?

People around the world, and across different religions, perceive God in many different ways. They understand Him based on the teachings they have received. This doesn't mean that one view is right and another is wrong; it simply means that our understanding is limited. God is so vast and magnificent that there's no way we could ever fully define Him.

## PS. Of PS.

To truly grasp this, we must first acknowledge that God, with His will and power, has created everything; from the tiniest to the grandest; and arranged it all in such a way that we might uncover a deeper meaning. If we come to understand this, we will at least become aware of the signs around us. Because we believe this arrangement is God's design, we begin to follow the signs, knowing they point toward a message.

In every language, there is a source of translation. In mathematics, it's infinity; in physics, it's energy; in chemistry, it's the atom; and in biology, it's the cell. I call it the Source. God is the name we have given to it, but everything traces back to the Source. The Source is the beginning of everything; an immense, powerful energy beyond description.

A higher intelligence, a superior talent, or a power greater than all of us, which is organized and oversees the order of the entire universe and galaxies. This theory may not have a scientific foundation; however, I firmly believe that there is, without a doubt, someone smarter, more genius, and stronger than us who has organized everything. This higher being has created all the natural forces of humanity; like trees, forests, the earth, and the sky; into this magnificent masterpiece.

now, this superiority, whatever name it may be called, can be anything. If you pay attention to these things, it means you've thought a bit, and you've stirred your awareness. By doing so, you're beginning to connect to a higher level of consciousness, frequencies, and information.

## (In other words)

The nucleus forms the core of an atom. It is singular and unique, with layers revolving around it. Each of these layers, depending on their proximity to the nucleus or their distance from it, has its own energy and movement. The layers closest to the nucleus are stronger, more stable, and more energetic than the others, and at times, they even provide energy to the subsequent layers. God is like that nucleus, the immense source of energy. He has a very strong frequency and positive energy and doesn't need the layers surrounding Him. It is the layers that depend on the nucleus to become more efficient. Perhaps having a positive frequency, willpower, and strength is related to how close one gets to the nucleus, in order to create a distinct core for themselves and become more efficient. Or, perhaps, the closer the energies get to their source, the more powerfully they revolve around the nucleus, and everything becomes more efficient.

## Gratitude

Every energy source is dependent on a larger source of energy, which is, in reality, the primary source from which it has been formed. We ignite our own energy from what is accessible to us, and now, to make this source more energized and efficient every day, we connect it to the primary source — which is God. all of us, as humans, fear emptiness. When we encounter a dead-end, we need a certainty that tells us nothing is pointless. Positive energy radiates more powerfully when it is nourished by the right source. What could be a better source than your own essence? as explained in Rhonda Byrne's book; The gratitude, clarifies all of this for us. Indeed, the miracle of gratitude is the best and most direct path to flooding your source with a large amount of positive energy all at once. The principle of gratitude is that you come to the belief that you are the best, and because of this belief, you give thanks. when you don't believe in yourself, you don't practice gratitude. therefore, the first step to gratitude is reconciling with yourself and believing in yourself. and how beautifully said Maulana: "Gratitude for a blessing increase that blessing." This blessing is the energy, and this energy consists of those small words you offer to yourself, and you thank yourself for generating this energy. The effects of this gratitude are so high that the results in life are far greater than any effort for mere survival. oh God, thank you for everything....


## In summary,

Accepting that life is not empty or worthless depends on our belief. Belief is the faith or conviction we have in ourselves and our God. To become confused, it is enough for your beliefs to be shaken. Without belief, you are merely a two-legged creature who lacks positive energy, or in other words, conscience. You won't attain that which is destined for you; humanity. Thus, in this way, you will drift further from your goal and bright future. Knowing your true essence; whether it is God, energy, or something else; helps you strive for yourself, make your energy positive, and, in turn, spread positive energy to others. This is the essence of humanity. Every day, you thank the Creator or the cause of your existence for the good feelings you have. For example, when your mother or spouse cooks a delicious meal for you, if you express your gratitude, they will cook something even better next time or at least maintain the same level of deliciousness. but if you say, 'What's this? Obviously, if you throw some meat into a pan, it will become delicious. What's so special about that, and why should I thank you?' I can assure you that next time, not only will you not get a delicious meal, but you might not even have anything to eat. perhaps you might ask, 'What kind of God needs us to thank Him?' It's not God's need for gratitude; it's our understanding and awareness that by showing gratitude, we become closer to Him. we strengthen our energy and frequency and become more thankful to ourselves. From this point onward, we can truly choose whether to live our lives meaningfully or waste our time. we must love ourselves and be in love with our Creator. otherwise, continuing will only be a waste of time. I had faith in my God and was at a stage where I needed to transform that faith into certainty, and this required logic. Loving myself and having faith in God was a feeling that I hadn't yet fully understood. I had to move beyond feeling and arrive at logic and certainty through thought.

# Chapter three

What things exist within me that I am unaware of?

With each passing day, I became more familiar with myself. It was as if I had just discovered who I truly was. I had only just begun to understand my own interests and tastes. There were things within me that felt foreign, things I had carried with me until that day that never truly belonged to me. I don't even know where they came from or why they had stayed with me. My inner world was filled with remnants left behind by others; things that were not mine. my irritability, my restlessness, my anxiety; they were all responses others had expected of me. None of them came from my own will or choice. I wasn't naturally an angry or aggressive person; or rather, I didn't use aggression as a tool. So, who or what had awakened this aggressive side of me? at that point in my life, I was so deeply immersed in making peace with myself that I couldn't bear the idea of anyone neglecting my inner being. When someone did, I would erupt in such rage and aggression that once I calmed down, even I would be shocked; where had that overwhelming and uncontrollable anger come from? why was it there? after some thought and reflection, I realized it was rooted in my past failures; in the times I had abandoned myself. I no longer wanted anyone to even slightly hurt me or to take me away from myself. But the way I tried to protect myself was completely wrong. It was like I was a child, throwing tantrums and pushing everyone away just to keep hold of a doll; terrified that someone might take it from me. yet in the end, that child isn't happy either, because after all the outbursts and pushing everyone away, they're left alone. I realized I had to protect my inner world by also gaining control over my outer world. and in order to do that, the first step was to journey into my own darkness;( those very parts of me that others had ignited). Life continued on its usual path. People, confused and distracted, were chasing after goals; both big and small. Meanwhile, I had found a sense of peace through reconciliation with myself and a hope rooted in God. I felt better. But the thoughts of my past, the memories and the events that occasionally resurfaced, seemed to contradict everything. I had collected my past memories; the ones carrying all those thoughts and emotions; and stored them away in a box, hoping to erase them from my mind. but it was as if I couldn't let them go. I had tucked that box into a corner of my mind, and every so often, I would go back and revisit the memories. but just one day of remembering could steal not only that day but more from me. because whenever I thought about those memories, all the emotions I had felt at that time would return with the same intensity. and after the wave of emotions, my thoughts would spiral. The things I hadn't said, the actions I hadn't taken; they all came rushing back. This overwhelming sense of having neglected myself would turn into a kind of self-hatred. every time I tried to free myself from those thoughts and memories, even in the best-case scenario, it would take days to recover. Out of habit, any small event in my life would trigger a return to the past, and I'd recall every painful experience I had lived through; and I'd feel even more exhausted than before. but now I had made peace with myself. I knew that in this land called "the world," I had a role to play; a role called "life." I didn't want to keep going as I had before, because I knew deep down it wasn't right. I was full of conditioning; shaped over time by my mother, father, school, university, and society. They had all influenced and molded me into who I had become, and I had rarely questioned any of it. Later on, even the people I spent time with, each of them had wanted something from me, and I had adapted myself to meet their expectations; not my own. within us are countless personalities and behaviors. Through our relationships, we draw out different aspects of ourselves and express them. which part of ourselves we activate depends largely on what the other person draws out or expects from us. our interactions with others are the most important factor shaping our behavior; something I'll explain further in the next chapter. I wanted to sculpt myself, to chip away at the surface and reach my own depths; to truly understand the meaning behind what I was seeing. So, the first step in this phase was to ask myself; Who am I?

Am I just a name? A child of my father? A servant of God? No; none of those roles could define me completely, especially since I hadn't chosen them myself. I didn't choose to be born to certain parents. I didn't choose my name. These things were never really mine to begin with. but one thing was certain: I was living this life by my own choice. and so, I had to know myself; this self I had only recently begun to like, but still didn't fully understand. I didn't know how this version of me had even come into being. Yet I deeply believed that life had placed me here, in this depth, for something far deeper. In this chapter of my life, I had begun to love myself; the very self I had long ignored. I had found the one person I had never truly cared for and it's me.

Once again, as I had so many times before, I began writing emails to myself, asking; Who am I? What do I love? What habits do I have? What are my strengths and weaknesses? It felt like getting to know someone new who had just entered my life; someone whose interests, opinions, and mindset I needed to understand. I asked myself questions with the intention of answering them mindfully. And at the end of the email, I added a note to myself;

Please, give the most honest answers; no sugarcoating.

I filled many pages, practicing and pouring out every thought and behavior I could recognize. for just seven days, I wrote down every recurring thought, habit, and behavior I noticed in myself. next to each one, I wrote down the reason behind it. I created a table where I listed my strengths and weaknesses, my good and bad habits. It wasn't easy, but I wrote everything truthfully.

By the time I reached the seventh page; now completely crumpled; I noticed that many of my behaviors had changed. I realized those changes were due to the environment I was in, or the people I was spending time with. Some behaviors had even disappeared entirely. That's when I understood; those behaviors weren't truly mine. they weren't the result of conscious choice or deep-rooted upbringing; they were simply reactions to the world around me. as a result, many of my thoughts began to change too; because once I understood the root of my thoughts, they would quickly lose their weight or meaning. but since these patterns had repeated in me for so long, they had become habits. and now, I had to break those habits. I quickly redrew my chart from scratch; two large columns; one for bad and negative habits, the other for good and positive ones. Under each, I listed my habits. you might not believe it, but in the "good habits" column, the only entry was; sending e-mail to myself. meanwhile, the "bad habits" column was completely full. I laughed; out loud. not out of embarrassment; actually, I felt curious, even eager to learn more. and I wrote that curiosity under my strengths. I read through everything carefully. Some habits; now right there on paper; made me feel ashamed. But at least now I understood them. some entries, like those under the "strengths" column, made me feel empowered. I wanted to fill up the "good habits" side; but how? I started by identifying the root of each bad habit. Every effect has a cause.

I had to find the reason behind each habit and the needs to fueled them; either to strengthen or eliminate them. So now, I asked myself; What was causing each bad habit? On a blank white sheet, I wrote down my bad habits. Then, using a different colored pen, I wrote the reason behind each one. I was now focused on solving the cause. If I could resolve the root issue, the habit; while difficult; could be changed. and if the problem couldn't be solved just yet, at the very least, I accepted it. I acknowledged that I had these bad habits and that the problem was mine; not someone else's. If I hit a dead end, I didn't blame others. It was up to me to live with that shortcoming. So, I accepted it.

And that acceptance brought me peace; the kind that comes from embracing yourself fully, with everything you are. even my flaws, once accepted, started to look beautiful. because anything that is accepted becomes beautiful. and in the end, I accepted myself with all my flaws and all my beauty. not to mention, the flaws that could be healed; I worked on them with practice and repetition, and gradually turned them into something beautiful too.

I began designing a personal behavioral blueprint for myself. I started to strengthen and practice the qualities I wanted to bring out from within; the parts of me I wished to express. What began as a mental sketch, I started to put into action, believing with full certainty that through repetition, these behaviors would eventually become my habits.

As for the negative habits I couldn't resolve; I accepted them. I became aware of their presence, though I kept them hidden.

This awareness helped me avoid environments where those negative patterns might resurface or be reinforced.

It also allowed me to recognize people who, whether knowingly or not, pulled me toward the darker parts of myself; and I learned to keep my distance from them, for days, even years if necessary.

Everyone has the potential to nurture good behavior, positive thoughts, and healthy habits. but at the same time, we're equally capable of causing harm and acting out darker impulses. that duality is part of human nature; it lives instinctively within us. we are the descendants of people who, in order to ensure their survival, did both noble and destructive things. so, those dark, hidden feelings lie quietly within us, often without our awareness. everything stays calm and silent; until we step on the wrong wire. then, that shadowy side of human nature can suddenly surface. the best among us isn't those who deny their flaws, but those who recognize their inner glitches, and choose to manage, suppress, or reshape them. that's where real awareness begins. when we understand our internal faults; our "bugs"; we can start to control our thoughts, and naturally, our behavior follows. and it's at that point that we begin to influence our environment, rather than letting it shape us. When you reach the point where you realize your thoughts are under your control, and you understand both your strengths and weaknesses, you begin to filter your thoughts. and through that, you allow the best version of yourself to emerge through your behavior. but this requires that you first recognize your inner bugs; the empty spaces, the unmet needs, the missing pieces of your personal puzzle. by addressing these inner gaps, you bring clarity to your thoughts. as your thoughts become clearer, your emotions naturally become more positive.

And then your behavior; shaped by both your emotions and your thoughts; starts to shift in ways you never thought possible. once you learn to control your thoughts and your emotions, you'll begin to strike a balance; a harmony between logic, which stems from the mind, and emotion, which springs from the heart. and it is at this very point that you begin to make the best choices.

The best decision is the one that balances both the mind and heart; a decision that stands at the center of that scale, perfectly weighed.

And I emphasize again: this kind of clarity only comes from deep self-awareness. once you truly know yourself, you become aware of the contents of your own mind; You know what thoughts live there, and you begin to consciously shape them, eliminating the ones that don't serve you. as a result, you start to experience clearer, more positive emotions, and with them, respectable behavior and better choices follow. this inner peace is the reward of knowing yourself; of suppressing negative habits and strengthening positive ones. when you fully understand yourself, you stop doing many of the things you used to do; because now, you recognize whether a thought, an emotion, or a behavior is fleeting, circumstantial, or simply a reflection of your environment or another person's expectations. you don't act impulsively anymore.

And the result of this mindful thinking in the moment is a reduced margin of error; a more conscious, intentional life.

**Postscript:**

How do we journey inward?

The simplest path; one that needs no class, no training, no cost; is to observe your thoughts. and don't identify with them. just watch them. don't take their side, and don't oppose them. be completely neutral, entirely non-judgmental. because the moment you judge, you give your thoughts an identity — you give them power. don't concern yourself with whether a thought is right or wrong.

your only task is not to offer any opinion. Just observe. If you stop feeding your thoughts with energy, what is true will reveal itself to you. and that truth; is what already exists within you. when you learn to enter the space of no-thought,

little by little, your identity, your mind, and your thoughts

will start to unfold before you.

### Post-Postscript

Knowing myself; and accepting it fully, with all its flaws and perfections;

is the greatest act I can do. deep within us, there is a soft, quiet whisper. If you become still, if you take even a small step back from the noise of the world,

you will be guided from that very place. when you are at peace,

when you are in a state of full acceptance, that is when God speaks to you.

(In Other Words) I wanted to express more gratitude.

When you truly taste the peace and power that comes with this inner state, your essence; especially if it seeks growth; naturally desires to amplify that energy. but to do so, you must first find your flaws. you've already discovered your strengths and given thanks for them. now, to reach higher levels of gratitude, you must increase the good within you. we've all, at some point, been shaped by the environments we've been placed in. unintentionally, we absorbed negativity, and without understanding its roots, we unknowingly strengthened it within ourselves. to me, every difficult thing begins to unravel the moment you know its source. once you understand why something became hard,

half the work is already done. Just like in school; remember?

Before solving a physics or math problem, we were taught to read and understand the question first. so, when you honestly list your strengths and weaknesses and write down the cause of each beside them, you're left with a cheat sheet; a life manual filled with hints for growth. you then enhance the causes behind your strengths, and begin to dissolve the causes of your weaknesses. and soon, you'll realize how much of your behavior has been shaped by the people and the places around you. at this point, you've not only found your light but also illuminated your shadows. now, you begin arranging your environment to support your growth and your peace;

and that is the greatest win of all. that's how you create a life with fewer mistakes and more serenity. our habits, actions, and traits

are either ones we've chosen to carry, or others have projected onto us through constant interaction. we were all born as pure and innocent beings.

What we carry now; it's our choice. Letting go of bad habits isn't as hard as it seems. Just try not doing them for a few days. understand their root. avoid the people or situations that feed them. and once you've developed self-awareness,

you'll naturally begin to explore deeper energy centers; what ancient Indian wisdom calls chakras, a word meaning "wheel" or "cycle."

After concentrating on the chakras, release your energy. When you direct your focus to each of the body's energy centers, all of your energy moves toward that particular area. You can activate these centers one after the other. For example, when you think of thirst, your mouth produces less saliva, and the areas of your tongue and jaw become dry—your body prepares you to drink cool water because the energy in that region has been activated.

Now, consider the unsaid points from your recent discussion. Your body secretes adrenaline, which occupies all your thoughts and mind. For now, just understand that the reason behind these events is that each energy center secretes its own specific hormone, which in turn activates the cells of the corresponding tissue or organ. If you learn to work with these centers, you will create a new level of energy in your mind, and the hormones will be secreted properly. By repeating this process consistently, you take control of your thoughts and hormones.

Now, let's review the body's energy centers:

The First Energy Center This center governs the sexual organs. The creative energy here is extremely potent, as it is designed for creating new life and the birth of a child. When this center is balanced, its creative energy flows within you.

The Second Energy Center, located in the area behind the navel, this center is responsible for functions such as nourishment, digestion, absorption, elimination, and so on. It can be seen as governing both preservation and release—the processes of consuming food and then eliminating it. When this center is in balance, you experience a sense of safety and security.

The Third Energy Center, situated in the abdominal cavity, this center governs the stomach, spleen, liver, and adrenal glands—the hormone associated with it being adrenaline. This center is responsible for decision-making, personal empowerment, anger control, and the ability to assert control over others. When it is balanced, you are endowed with the willpower and perseverance necessary to overcome environmental challenges and difficulties.

Forth Energy Center; located behind the chest, this chakra governs the heart and lungs. Its related hormone is the thymus, which plays a key role in strengthening the immune system. this center is the home of emotions such as love, compassion, gratitude, empathy, and humanity. many of the divine qualities within us emerge from here; because this is the seat of the soul. when this chakra is balanced, a person lives with love, shows kindness to others, and experiences a deep sense of inner wholeness.

fifth Energy Center; located in the throat area, this chakra governs the thyroid gland and neck. the hormones related to it are thyroid hormones, which regulate the body's metabolism. this center is associated with expression, honesty, speaking your truth, and the ability to communicate clearly. when this chakra is in harmony, your voice becomes the voice of truth, and you can express your thoughts and emotions with ease and confidence.

sixth Energy Center; This chakra is found behind the forehead and the throat area, linked to the pineal gland – often referred to as the third eye. It is responsible for intuition, inner vision, lucid dreams, and awareness beyond the five physical senses. when activated, this center leads you to a higher level of perception and insight.

Seventh Energy Center; located at the top of the head, it governs the pituitary gland – also known as the master gland, which controls all other endocrine glands in the body. When this center is balanced, one reaches a state of complete harmony between mind, body, and spirit, and experiences a deep connection to higher consciousness and inner light.

8th Energy Center; this chakra lies about 40 centimeters above the head and is not connected to the physical body. It is the source of our connection to the universe, the divine, and the infinite energy of creation. when this center is active and in balance, you experience a deep, undeniable sense of worthiness, fulfillment, and divine purpose.

The purpose of introducing these chakras was to familiarize you with what exists within you; to show how much neglecting ourselves can lead to pain and misdirection from the right path. maybe I used the chakras as a metaphor for my writings, to express how important this chapter truly is. to emphasize that deep self-knowledge is a major achievement on the path toward what you truly desire.

Now; by making peace with yourself, by recognizing your flaws and imperfections and working to complete them, by becoming aware of your inner energy centers; you can transform your life. you don't necessarily need meditation, yoga, or 369 Hz frequencies to open your chakras.

Sometimes, just thinking deeply can; seventh chakra - Your eye opens to the truth of life, as it truly is. the sixth -You speak truthfully and with integrity. the fifth -You fall in love with yourself first, and then others. the fourth – You gain self-control and make powerful, wise decisions. the third – You feel a deep sense of security. the second- You are ready to give life to something or someone else. the first – and finally, with the eighth chakra, you feel worthy, peaceful, and fulfilled; without needing to perform extraordinary acts. you simply exist as you are, and that is more than enough – eighth chakra.

## In Summary:

If you become aware of all the things you've cultivated within yourself, and you begin to organize them, then you are ready for the awakening of the chakras; meaning awakening of awareness.

Now, what happens if we engage all of these energy centers?

First, we direct the creative energy of the first chakra along the intended path. If we feel secure enough and tap into our creative power, this evolved creative energy rises to the second energy center. we use this energy to overcome limitations and challenges in our environment. then the energy moves to the third center; the seat of willpower and strength. After successfully overcoming our challenges, we experience a sense of wholeness and satisfaction. as the energy reaches the fourth center, we begin to feel love for ourselves and others, and our true identity starts to take form. what we have learned from love and completeness is then expressed, and this enriched energy flows into the fifth energy center. once the sixth energy center is activated by this evolved energy, the dormant areas of the brain awaken; the veil is lifted from our eyes, and we confront reality. when we feel complete balance and harmony at this level, the energy enters the seventh center and activates it. Our external environment becomes more aligned with us, and we experience a deep sense of worth; leading us into the eighth center, where we see the results of our inner work.

All of this growth and evolution is only possible if we; Recognize and understand our flaws and shortcomings. Avoid being influenced by past thoughts or external environments that can trap our energy. Work toward inner completion, correct our imperfections, and forgive and accept ourselves. Only then can we allow these centers to exchange energy freely; or better yet, take control of this energetic exchange ourselves.

# Chapter Four

One day, I woke up and tasted the true essence of love

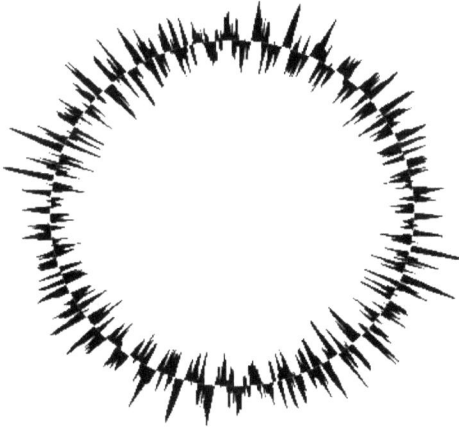

This chapter of my life was filled with many tests from God; both to prove to myself that I was on the right path and, as someone who wanted to share this path with others, to demonstrate that the choice I had made was the right one. I went through so many intense and diverse experiences that honestly; one chapter is not enough. I even wrote a novel about all of it, which is now ready for publication. But here, I'll briefly share how these changes helped me; and at times, challenged me deeply.

When I had no one to talk to, I found companionship in myself. I fell in love with who I was and raised my own energy. Right in that moment of self-exploration, when I was enjoying who I had become and what I had created, I felt the desire to share my time with someone else.

Maybe I had become too lost in the outer world; I wanted to build a little cabin for two, with all the energy I had cultivated within myself. I met a stranger who somehow felt familiar. I lived in a time when striving to simply be human felt like a painful struggle. The world was full of cruelty and bizarre schemes among people; the one who acted cruelly faster was the one who "won," while those who had been hurt turned into something else entirely... and that transformation kept spreading, like a virus of darkness and bitterness.

People my age were chasing empty, shallow things, getting high off risky and fleeting pleasures. They thought they were winning. I'm not saying everyone, but most people put themselves in positions where they could take advantage of others. Without a doubt, they were a bunch of lost souls; unaware of who they were, either trying to steal someone else's identity or destroy it. If I hadn't caught myself in time, I might've ended up as one of them too. But I chose differently; I strengthened my roots for survival. It was fascinating to me that, in this day and age, someone in their twenties wouldn't even think about their roots. Without realizing it, they were wasting their time chasing things that were never meant to last. This fear of people; this dread of such a reality; pushed me into solitude. I preferred being alone over being surrounded by people who were emotionally unwell. But then, I reached a feeling I hadn't touched in years. I felt that with the energy and power I had cultivated, maybe I could awaken a feeling in my heart strong enough to make my brain release serotonin.

So, I found the courage to spend time with someone.

He was extremely busy and preoccupied, trying to build a life where he could have more freedom of choice; without taking even a moment to think about himself. In the chaos of his fake surroundings, all he was doing was adding shine to the surface of his life. Still, there was something about him that intrigued me, something that drew me in. Despite all that glitter, his eyes lacked joy. He was desperately searching for himself; perhaps unknowingly, or maybe he did know.

After a few meetings and not-so-deep conversations, I realized that a kind of affection was beginning to form. I talked to him about loving myself, about God, and energy. He listened carefully.

My personality beside him became exactly the one I had designed in my solitude. And now, like an architect, I was bringing those designs to life. I wanted to spend more time with him so I could reveal the hidden halves of myself; parts that, until then, had only existed on paper.

It was like a theater where I had written the script myself and played the only role. And now I had the chance to perform my own monologue, hoping that I; the director as well; would approve. It was sweet that his excitement over my behavior encouraged me to perform even better.

I wasn't acting or lying; it was just that after all the transformation I had gone through, I had no co-star for my story. That's when I started telling myself: maybe this is the turning point in my story; maybe God sent this person so I could give the performance of a lifetime. I wanted to win my own award.

My partner was a wealthy person who put a lot of effort into making his life stylish and luxurious. And somehow, he considered my behavior and presence part of that luxury; as if I had become a "luxury" myself. That's when I realized; I had become refined. I knew myself well. I had mastered myself. This stage of my life was a test; like a child who just learned to walk, wobbly but on the right path. And his arrival? It taught me how to run, even if he didn't know it. In those moments, I regretted not having had all of this sooner. But then I realized; the reason this person showed up now was because I was finally on the right path. I hadn't just found my path; I had chosen it.

At that point in my life, I had developed myself so much that I wasn't looking for a "missing half" anymore, but for a "lost companion." I knew myself; my strengths, my weaknesses. I had accepted those flaws, and through self-love, I had attracted him. Even when he pointed out my flaws, I could listen with calm because I knew exactly where they were and accepted them. And sometimes, when he made unfair criticisms, I defended myself confidently and explained my perspective. That's when I understood; the people who come into our lives; good or bad; are reflections of the parts of ourselves we may not even be aware of. How can you walk through a barren desert and not run into bandits?

If we heal the ugliness and emptiness within us, we'll make better choices. Otherwise, we'll keep chasing our inner voids; the dark corners of our soul. If I had the wrong people in my life, it was because I was wandering down the wrong path; or to put it better, because I carried the wrong habits within me and followed them. But now, I am still the same person, just with one difference: I've found myself. Gradually, I got used to being present; to the stability of my character and to the bright spots that had long been hidden in the shadowed half of my being. Maybe it sounds selfish, but I loved him for myself. I needed him to be. This feeling led me to understand the true meaning of love.

Love is not about self-sacrifice; it's about self-realization.

Love relies on the beautiful things inside you. Once you recognize them, you project them outward; and they come back to you like a reflection in a mirror.

Love isn't about not reaching your beloved; it's about reaching yourself *with* your beloved.

Love isn't about suffering; it's about seeing the bright side of your being, the one you've uncovered.

I now challenge everything I had read and heard in books;

Love is the good feeling someone gives you; a feeling that brings out your best self and helps you discover your inner world. Love is the teacher who reveals your greatest and most hidden talents. To me, love is the journey to yourself; and ultimately, to God.

Love makes you kind, and kindness is God.

Love doesn't make you crazy; it makes you wisely yourself.

Love sets your soul free so it can fly back home; to your being, not to get hurt. Love is when the mere sight of your beloved makes you thank God unconsciously. Love is like an unexpected guest arriving at your door. And when you know where everything is in your house; when you know what the best of yourself is; you offer it to that guest. You just need to be a good host. I knew what was beautiful within me. I brought it out, showed it, and not only did he enjoy it; I did too. That inspired him to invite me into his world. And in return for my hospitality, he prepared the best of himself to offer me. Unintentionally, he was inviting me to myself; and I was consciously introducing him to the bright side of his being. I helped him see himself, recognize his flaws and heal them, and strengthen his virtues. and because he, like every human, should love himself, the closer he got to knowing himself, the more grateful he became to me; and the more he fell in love with me.

What he didn't realize was that he had fallen in love with himself beside me; and to stay in love with himself, he needed me. our life together truly began when we both gained emotional stability. The feeling that we were two whole people; complete beside each other; made us realize that we shouldn't separate. We decided to walk the remaining path of life together. how beautiful it is; the true meaning of love and seeing the reality of life.

Love is that peace born in your heart, sent to your brain; and your brain's reaction shows up in your behavior.

If that doesn't happen, my friend, you haven't experienced love; you've lived ignorance.

---

## Postscript:

Love is like an arrow aimed at the *mind*, not the heart.

It's the mind that stays; the heart can break.

## Post-Postscript:

All of us need someone who brings us closer to ourselves;

someone who makes us love ourselves more.

That is love. anything else is disaster. If you can love yourself, transform yourself, and fall in love with your Creator, then you are capable of loving someone else; and wishing for them what you wish for yourself. You help them make peace with who they are.

That is to fall in love; and to make someone fall in love.

## (In other words) I sought love to teach the art of loving.

At this stage, I finally answered the questions I had in the first stage. Honestly, it made me laugh; or better to say, I was embarrassed.

How was I searching for love with such an empty energy tank and complete disregard for myself?

I had nothing to offer; no energy to exchange. Love is an earthly energy that functions like an electroscope; a device used to detect electric charges.

Now that I wholeheartedly loved myself and expressed gratitude for it, I began seeking someone who could measure the positive charge within me; so that we could exchange these positive energies. everyone, whether they're aware of it or not, seeks positive energy and is attracted to it. when you have a visible, tangible source of positive energy, people who crave it are drawn to you; at the very least to feed off the transcendent energy you've created within yourself. But here's the beauty: by feeding off your energy, not only is your energy *not* depleted; it actually grows stronger.

And they too learn from you; consciously or not; how to raise their own energy.

In this mutual process, they end up helping you further nourish your own energy. you might ask; but what if they suffocate that energy?

Here's the reassurance; when you're on the right path, operating at high frequencies with strong, clear energy, there's *no such thing* as the wrong person entering your path. Your energy acts as a steel boundary, repelling negative people. This is when you truly experience love; and no longer fear the kind of "love" that was once poisoned by negativity and fear. Love will bring an abundance of positive energy into your life;

but you can only experience this kind of love after completing the three stages before it.

It was exactly when I was in love with myself that I fell in love with him.

To reach a shared belief and build a new future, we must have a clear goal and a higher emotional intention. when your heart is at peace, it sends that peace to your mind, and the mind, in turn, reflects this state throughout the body.

Your heart, aligned with the deep inner source within you, finds peace with the person beside you. when your heart and mind work in harmony, you always feel fulfilled. at this point; once you've understood the true meaning of love;

you feel whole. No more emptiness. because you've met your ideal self, and you're living a brand-new experience. based on what I explained in the previous chapter, the fourth energy center begins in the heart.

this energy is deeply connected to the feeling of self-actualization.

Such a feeling can create peace; not only within, but also between you and the world around you. when this energy center opens, we encounter other positive emotions such as: forgiveness, service, compassion, love, and trust. and here, we begin to experience completion.

In this section, I want to explore the importance of the heart (love); and how it influences our lives, thoughts, and emotions. The heartbeat occurs independently of the brain and the nervous system, yet it still works in harmony with them. Therefore, any change in the nervous system directly affects the heart's rhythm. every emotion; whether conscious or unconscious; affects your heartbeat, and these changes are directly transmitted back to the nervous system. now you may begin to understand the importance of the person beside you. The one who can help align your heartbeat to a rhythm that, once sent to the brain, brings peace to your being. that rhythm is the love for the Self. Love; the motivation to connect with your inner truth; creates a coherent and steady rhythm in your body. because our emotions directly influence the functioning of our hearts at every moment, if we awaken the heart with elevated emotions, its energy will influence the body's entire functioning. the emotions you radiate from your heart place the brain under your control. and the brain, in turn, governs your body; your present, and your future. so, arriving at the core of your being and loving yourself; especially in the presence of someone who supports that journey; is a powerful step toward creating your ideal future. when you take these truths seriously, you'll begin to let go of relationships, thoughts, and anything that distorts your emotions (heart) and thoughts (mind).

Because you realize: these things are the chains holding you back from your desired future. real change happens when your thoughts are aligned with your emotions. and in such a state; if your partner can no longer walk beside you, for any reason; you no longer feel despair. Instead, you accept their absence with peace, because the energy and frequency you've worked so hard to build will not fade. and instead of losing, you begin to gather yourself more deeply, organizing your energy to guide your thoughts and emotions toward the future you truly desire.

## In Summary

One very important thing is that, in order to maintain better balance, you must always prioritize love for yourself first, then love for God, and then love for your beloved. This love triangle must always follow this order; otherwise, you will face things that are completely out of your control. when you spend time improving your energy and showing gratitude to your Source, you build a strong reserve of positive energy that you can then share with someone else; your beloved. otherwise, you become subject to the influence of the other person. They begin to dictate which parts of you should shine and which should remain hidden. In that state, you become like clay, shaped by someone else's hands. If, for any reason; whether intentional or not; they awaken your darker parts, you may lose your love for God through resentment and sorrow. your inner self, with all its energy, begins to fade and be forgotten. never forget; Falling in love has prerequisites. you must first be in love with yourself, and in love with God. only after passing these stages can, you truly fall in love with another. repeat this practice daily; before admiring your beloved, be grateful for yourself and for God. this feeling gives you the power to take charge of energy exchange in the relationship.

When you fully restore and understand yourself, fulfill your own needs, and love yourself sincerely; while remaining grateful to your Creator; you will discover a love that is true. at this moment, you must stand firm in your personality and not change for anyone. you must be aware of both the dark and light parts within you, so that when you choose to express them, it is on your own terms. If you're unstable at this stage, you will be changed; into someone you never were, shaped by someone else's vision of you. and you will be left with a version of yourself you don't recognize. that's why you fail; because you lost yourself and your connection with God through someone to whom you gave your love. and when you no longer want to fail, you keep walking with that damaged or reshaped version of yourself, once again letting others mold you. So, before changing, think deeply about who you truly are; how beautiful and complete you already are. get so close to yourself that you can hold yourself tightly in your own arm; so, no one can take that away from you.

In that state, you become the brightest version of yourself. and someone who is worthy of that version will cherish it by your side. that's when you understand the true meaning of love. never forget; you are beautiful through the self that you've built from within; not from the outer image shaped by others.

# Chapter Five

How can we create a new life and destiny for ourselves?

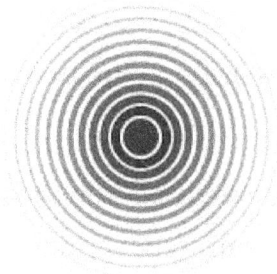

The time has come to say goodbye to your past self. I know it's hard; because you're about to leave behind one of the strongest versions of yourself. A version that has walked deep into the darkness, stayed with you for years, and returned once again to the light. That same version of you is the one that awakened you on your path to awareness. But now is the time to let that version blossom. You've fought hard to become the future version of yourself, and your past self doesn't like that. Let it go. Just allow yourself to see the future with what you've built.

Everything started to take on a new meaning for me. I was still living in a time when reading wasn't common, ignorance had fans, and trickery would win. But those things had died in my world. Life was so much more than something to ruin with those traits. I knew I was on the right path, and sooner or later, everyone would join this path. So once again, I started emailing myself. And after praising, thanking, and sometimes even scolding myself, I asked one question:

What is life?

So many words and sentences poured into my mind that I couldn't even focus enough to explain it in one sentence. But to understand, I had to grasp the essence. Maybe life is the memories, or the constant worries.

Or maybe it's an illusion of the future, daydreams and fantasies. So then where is the *now* in life? Life truly has a deep meaning, and understanding it takes time. Reaching the point of truly asking "What is life?" required all those emails, and faith in a higher power that created me, and trust in that power; because I knew nothing meaningless comes from Him. I had gone through those stages and started wondering: What is my life? So that with the changes I've made now, I can transform my life too.

Before trying to describe life with the clichés that thousands before me have said over the decades; back when we didn't even exist; I realized that the more I studied, the more I understood; to live, first you need to know what life is. Think of it like this: "If you don't know where the clutch, brake, or gas pedal is in a car; or when and why you need to shift gears; you'll never be able to drive." We are that car. And living is like driving. You need to know the parts of the car and how it moves to drive. And to become a better driver, you even need to know the flaws of the car; so if it breaks down somewhere, you won't be stranded. Now that you know how the car moves, you're ready to travel toward your chosen path or destination. Yes, life is just that, a machine that is at my disposal, and the only thing I have control over. The word opportunity was the most important part of this sentence, so life is an opportunity that is available to me through choosing my path and understanding myself to reach my goals. Life is the opportunity for me to achieve my desires. Can an opportunity be missed? So, life is my understanding of opportunity. If I did not know myself and did not believe in my God, I would give my opportunity to someone else to live for me, or perhaps take my life away. Now it was time for me to determine my destination with all my might, relying on myself, which I had mastered, and find the closest way to reach it. Changing thoughts is the same as changing direction and changing life. Life is my thoughts. This sentence is very profound; the thoughts that have taken residence in my mind, where did they come from, why have they remained, what feelings do they give my heart, and what reactions do they provoke in my behavior, and this behavior causes certain beings to stay or leave my side, as all of these encompass my life. If these thoughts are correct, I can take my opportunity into my hands and live... To validate this sentence, just ask yourself: How is your life? A part of memories, people, and environments flows to your brain. Without blaming yourself, you see their impacts on your life, which may be the cruelest thing possible. Can you hand over your life to others while you can control it yourself? Self-control means controlling thoughts... Open your thoughts, do all your thoughts help you that you have placed in your mind... To zoom in on your thoughts more precisely, the first step is to clear your memories, let go of the memories that influence your thoughts. At this stage, you will see how few thoughts are in your mind that you can clean. Now that you have filtered your thoughts, look at what remains... Which of them helps you to start, which one empowers you and gives you hope? If none of these remain in your filter, do not be afraid, filter your thoughts again... Keep doing this until the only thing that remains is a strong positive thought, even if it is just one thought; that is acceptable. In this moment, you give that thought wings, you enlarge it, and you send the feeling of this thought as energy into your being or your heart, and this energy is sent back to your brain. You have received the answer from your powerful thought, and now you arrange the circumstances to be closer to your thoughts. Circumstances mean the environment you are in and the people you associate with. Now, you will create experiences in your serious environment, which you have already provided to your brain; it will seek it out, and through trial and error, you will find your path. And at this stage, life begins; just continue your path calmly and freely and take advantage of your opportunities along the way... If you have heard sentences like "life is very simple" or "life is shorter than that," etc., they are talking about the stage afterward, not that we should pride ourselves in our ignorance, feeling good about our emotions and behaviors without understanding our essence and consciousness. Awareness is not an unbelievable, strange, or distant thing; it is just enough to know ourselves and our thoughts a little.

Postscript

You were born in different worlds for different things. If you miss the opportunity, there is no longer a world that belongs to you.

Post-postscript

Life has given me the chance to understand, to love, and to reach higher levels. I don't know why, but this opportunity is my life. I want to live again and again, so I won't miss my chance and believe that life is my opportunity to reach my mission.

(In other words)

Life is a quantum field that wants to bring my energy into the flow.

The quantum field is an invisible field of energy and information. This field exists beyond time and space. It is a place where you will not observe any physical or material items; therefore, it is beyond the understanding of your senses. At this stage, we see the vibrations of previous stages; if we live with our own vibration or frequency (that is, reinforcing the source energy) close to the vibration and frequency of life, this is where we establish a union with life that results in success. Now, if this vibration or frequency is different from each other, it is the peak of catastrophe, and we become dangerously radioactive. Life is beyond the understanding of our senses, so to experience it, we comprehend a small part of it for ourselves. We must simply reach the understanding that this life is the opportunity we want to spread the energies we've drawn around ourselves so that we can move with the power of this energy in this quantum field. Now that I have cleared my energies, I must come to the certainty that life has provided me with an opportunity to get moving and reach my goal with the power of the energy and frequency that I have chosen. At this stage, do you still consider life to be futile and silly, merely for wasting time? No, on the contrary, at this stage, you look at your lifespan and stress about making the best use of the remaining opportunity, and now you strengthen your energy and resources more than before because you need them to move. One day, you decided to reconcile with yourself and chose good habits, and now you determine your path with the opportunity you have.

Now that we have come to the conclusion that life is our opportunity to reach our mission, we seize the opportunity and do whatever is necessary to utilize our chance. I have spent my time on awareness that is like an experienced elderly person teaching all my writings and thoughts; although lonely and considered ill, as I mentioned earlier, this is not a disease but a health that the general society needs because I found the true meaning of being human through small and simple exercises that anyone can understand, not as a philosopher with bizarre theories nor as a scientist with extraordinary discoveries; rather, I was an individual with everyday failures that many of us encounter; yet by understanding and controlling our experiences, we can achieve a positive impact of awareness for living and register a new memory for ourselves. Remember that our life is precisely our thoughts, memories, and recollections.

How can we create a new life and destiny for ourselves? The first step is to step out of the path we have been living on so far, clear our memories, and think about a great position for ourselves.

We have experienced things in life and recorded the emotions resulting from these experiences in our memory, and when we encounter similar events, we understand the same emotions we previously stored in memory; thus, we go back to the past. If these emotions we have stored in our memory dominate our thoughts, you cannot think beyond what you are; thus, you become a prisoner of the past and continuous repetition. Up to today, we have given our minds instructions and have lived according to them. Now that we have changed our energy, frequency, and vibrations, it is time to end our past life, which lacked these frequencies and vibrations, and create a new life with them.

Now it is time for you to give instructions to your mind. Control your mind to move toward the new things that we will create for ourselves. If you pay attention to your thoughts throughout the day, you will realize that you are living in the past, not the present, and you may be predicting a future for yourself. Now that you have taken your energy from the outer world and focused it on the inner world, you are creating a strong field of energy around your body and have the necessary energy to create anything new. Don't be surprised if your thoughts return to old places; because your thoughts are impatient and restless, always wanting to take action and be active; this is the memory you have given them. You take control of these thoughts through practice and repetition, and by overcoming daily habits, you elevate your willpower. Focus all your attention and thought on the present moment as if your mind is a blank slate that has not felt any bad memories or experiences. When you move to the present, you teach your body how to resonate with the new mind.

**In summary,**

when you learn to eliminate your memories, your life, and pointless relationships with any person at any place and time, and release the energy trapped in the past that has remained like a seal in your mind, you control your energy and frequency and move toward the future you desire. Reaching the present time simply requires us not to think about the past and the thoughts entangled with it. Set aside thoughts about troublesome memories of people and topics so as not to awaken old energies, and continuously focus on what we are now and, in another corner of our mind, the future we want (we will explain in the next chapter). Now we are in the sweet moment of the present, and we have abundant positive energy and blessings to control our mind. We have made all our frequencies and vibrations positive. Our mind is not disturbed or entangled in the sweet and bitter memories of the past and is intertwined with what we want, guiding us toward the desired future.

# Chapter Six

That was not just a dream.

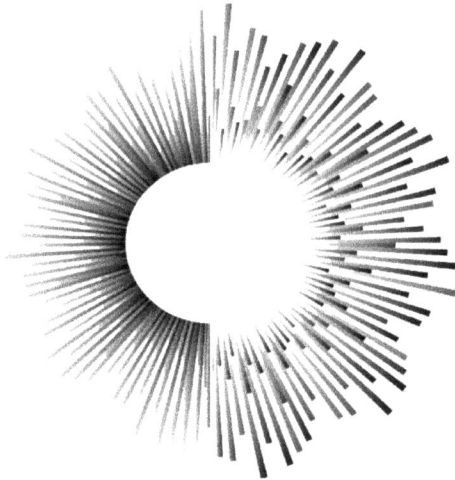

One day when I woke up, I was caught up in a dream that I had seen in my sleep. A dream that was not like an ordinary dream. A real sensation accompanied by a smell and taste that I felt even in waking. I forced my eyes shut to see my dream again; but it was ineffective. I had always believed that my dreams lead to reality; but this was a dream that had awakened me, so I knew I could achieve it. Perhaps the timing was a bit distant, but no, the timing was in my hands. I decided to turn my dream into a goal and reach it, so it was no longer just a dream but my goal. I wrote down papers for it, trying to focus as much as possible and bring all the details to paper, and this was the hardest task imaginable; because I had only achieved it in my dreams and had not seen a way of how and in what manner to reach it; so I started sketching the path of the dream that had now become my goal.

The easier the goal became, the less excitement there was about reaching it; every day I postponed it, thinking that I would do it the next day; because reaching it was easy. But my goal was much more difficult than I wanted to give seconds to minutes; but my goal was perfectly clear. I wrote it on paper as if I had just reached it. I wanted to check with myself whether it was as sweet as I had seen in the dream or not? It was so sweet for me that my pen and paper had become worn out. My goal was not something transcendental and unclear; but why did it seem like a dream now? Because I was far from it. Now I stepped back a bit and came out of the excitement of reaching it, looking at the paper and thinking about what I should do to reach the moment that had made me all sweet.

I was drawing labyrinthine paths for it, crumpling the papers and tossing them around to arrive at a result. Sometimes it crossed my mind that this was madness and that it had only been a dream; but I quickly focused my thoughts and stubbornly examined what I wanted on this path, how much I had to invest, and be persistent. Finally, after much effort, I wrote the desired path and had 001 items at the top. Out of sheer fatigue, I reached the warm embrace of the bed and the energizing hands that were waiting for me on the bed.

In the morning when I woke up, there was no sign of the constant rolling on the bed. This time I did not wake up on my own. I had made myself a slave to the clock beside my bed to cruelly force me with its rough sound to wake up quickly from the bed that was an enemy to me and to quickly reach some water and start walking on the path of my goal. Following my usual routine, I completed my gratitude and rummaged through my bookshelves to acquire the necessary awareness of my goal. Among the shelves were unrelated things that made it hard for me to find the book I was looking for. I started reading and gaining awareness. Each passing day, I learned things that perhaps did not advance me forward; but I made myself strong and solid to see the steps ahead; like someone who wants to travel somewhere. First, they examine the maps of that place to find the closest and least dangerous route. I examined them with as much care as possible. Because I knew that traveling carries risks, your vehicle might get a flat tire, you might get stuck in a desert without water and food, and in the forest where you wander, a big bear might charge at you. I had to explore ways to cope with those situations and learn. This alone made me feel alive, and I was human and in pursuit of survival. I read and learned with greater force and did trial and error. Whatever your goal may be, you must first prepare yourself. A runner, to reach the finish line of a race, first trains, strengthens their legs, focuses on their muscles, and after warming up their body, checks the route and then starts running as fast as they can to reach the finish line. Concentrate so precisely on yourself and strengthen your muscles like that runner so that you have no weakness, then with as much care as possible, using all the power of your sight, check the path, find shortcuts, correct your navigation service and put it in your ear, take the necessary tools with you, and even prepare for unfortunate events. Once you have done these things correctly, take the navigator in your hand and start.

Perhaps on the path you took, you did not reach the intended destination and sat along the way to enjoy; but at least the fact is that you have gone to the best place in your life; like the book "The Alchemist," you traveled to reach your destination, which is yourself.

To reach this stage of life, I emphasize again that I had to complete the previous steps, it had become a habit for me and I could easily control my thoughts. I thought so clearly and realistically about what I wanted that I imagined myself in that position, energy flowed towards me that truly fortified me as if I had already reached my goal. I knew that whatever I constantly thought about, I would attract it; before clearing my thoughts, I was exactly attracting the very thoughts I feared would happen to me, but now my conditions had changed. I had given so much wings and space to all my positive thoughts that my emotions were lifting me up. I was experiencing it and I knew that sooner or later, I would attract it... Once my thoughts changed, as I mentioned in the previous chapter, my environment and my surroundings also changed. Now that I knew what my goal was, I had arranged everything and everyone so that I would reach my goal as quickly as possible; even my Google searches had changed... Everything was reminding me of reaching and getting closer... Maybe the simplest and least costly way for your desire is to visualize it realistically and in the way it is supposed to happen, feel its essence, taste its flavor; unconsciously even your body becomes straighter under the influence of your thoughts, you become stronger and more confident, so first of all, you must align your energy with your goals and then attract it. Bring your frequency closer and closer to the frequency of what is meant to happen for you, so that when you reach your desire, you already feel its energy and frequency.

Now, living in any situation you are in is enjoyable; because you have understood the meaning of life, you have found yourself in the best way, and you have a goal that you have set out for, and if necessary, you will fight for it. We did not come to this world in vain. Hidden within this life are secrets, and this path must reach a correct destination for us to understand the story. Rest assured that God has given you enough time to reach your path; if you have strayed from your path, there is still hope for reaching your goal. For greater preservation and care, it will take you to where you can reach your goal.

## Postscript

In order to achieve your goal, you must focus on it, calm your mind, and simply find the path to reach it.

## Post-Postscript

Being aware of the path makes it less risky and brings you closer to your goal. Now you understand that controlling your thoughts means controlling your actions, controlling your actions means controlling your choices and path, and controlling these means reaching the final destination. You are closer to your goal at this stage of your life than ever before because everything is in the right place. I did what I needed to live my dream; to turn your possibilities into reality, you must have a clear goal and altered emotions; that is, you need to know clearly and specifically what you really want. Describe all the details carefully. When you focus your thoughts on what you want and consider all aspects, these thoughts act like electrical charges that send you directly to the quantum field. Now that you've clearly stated your intention and purpose, intertwine your emotions with this intention. Taste the pleasure and excitement it brings as if you have achieved your desire. When you do this, your emotions send out such a positive frequency that brings you closer to your desires, and this allows you to feel the transformation of your heart, brings order and coherence to your mind, and with this frequency and vibrations, you attract your desire, no additional efforts are needed. When you can visualize your desire and outline a future for yourself, your mind sees the future and must let go of the past. Release all problems related to depression and frustration, visualize the future you think about, and bring your emotions closer to it so they can resonate and attract powerfully. As I mentioned in the previous chapter, when you forget your past, past emotions like fear, anger, etc. fade away. These emotions lower your vibration and cannot help you create the right thoughts for beautiful future dreams. The more you strengthen positive emotions, the higher your energy, frequency, and vibration will be. Thus, the energy that radiates from you will be stronger, more magnificent, and more pervasive, impacting your life. The issue you need to consider is that you should not choose the timing for your desires to manifest. This will take you back to past solutions. The same old emotions will come alive again, and the usual image of your life will be illuminated once more. You just need to remember that every time you see your future with energy in the present moment, you bring the future one step closer to yourself. When you are on a new level of energy, you will experience new frequencies. Try to visualize your future realistically and naturally, just as you intend to live in the future, and the most important thing is that you have already experienced the feelings and energy of your future. Praise the divine force within you, open your heart, and be grateful for your bright future from now on.

**(In other words)** the goal is the same: reaching the source of energy, only the paths to get there are different.

The arrangement is a correct arrangement. In my opinion, a person makes the right decision when they are in absolute calm, and today, you are immersed in inner and outer peace. Now, you decide which path to choose to reach the otherworldly energy known as success. Our essence is designed in such a way that we have a strong desire to achieve success. This success is different for everyone based on their desires; but ultimately, the goal is one: "to be successful." Being successful means creating conditions where your peace is not disturbed and preparing conditions to become a source of energy. The path to success is circular; that is, your starting and ending point are the same, with the difference that you are now closer to the core (the true energy of God). If you remember, the hardest layer we wanted to separate from the core was the closest layer. A success that is arranged in this way is invincible because you have become so powerful from within that all external events are under your control, and with greater awareness, you chose a less dangerous path, and nothing can bring you down. Now, you have turned into a superhuman, the intermediary for channeling absolute energy to the earth.

In summary, what you think produces energy in the environment, and if you repeat this thought, it creates a physical result in your life. You act according to how you think, and your actions return to you. As I said, your thoughts are our life; your thoughts are the future you give yourself. If you constantly think about negative things, the result of your work and what you expect will be a negative disaster. So, positive thoughts about your goals and positive words about yourself are very effective steps in your future. You are always the cause and effect of your life... The mind is a powerful resource that is a gift from God to us. Perhaps all the answers to our questions are stored within it, and we just need to reflect a little. This task requires the absence of empty and futile thoughts... Organizing thoughts is a significant achievement in life. It is your thoughts that give you direction on which way to move.

# Chapter Seven

## The mission of life

(Dharma)

Today was the day I reached that dream. It was exactly as I had seen years ago in a dream, with the same grandeur and the same sweetness that had engulfed my entire being. I felt a different sensation that I had never experienced before, a feeling that I think should be called the seventh sense. My feeling of awakening at that moment was exactly like years ago when I woke up from the dream, and now that that dream had become reality, I awakened at that moment. I was scared because I hadn't paved the way forward, and now what should I do? Where should I go? Who am I? The one who had started this journey bore no resemblance to the person I had become at the end of the journey, or rather at the peak of my life. I was both estranged from myself and in a place where I was. You must have seen strangers after just a few words of conversation and felt as if you had known them for years; I was exactly like that with myself. I had never thought about this part of my life, I had thought about the moment of reaching my goal for days, and perhaps seconds; but not about its continuation. I felt that now the curtain of my life should be drawn on the stage of my life, and I should come to an end; but life continued to flow. From the peak where I stood, I could see people, but they could not see me. Some were so far away that to my eyes they appeared like black ants.

Some were spinning around themselves at the foot of the mountain and getting tired, throwing themselves to the ground. Some were grabbing the feet of a person who was struggling to pull themselves up the slope to climb higher, while others ruthlessly threw many large stones behind them to make the path more difficult for the next ones. I, standing up there, wanted to draw their attention and call everyone to listen to them so I could teach them; but my voice couldn't reach. I looked up and the light was much closer to me than the days I walked on Earth. I could even see the manifestation of the rays of light. The path behind me was the same path I had taken to reach the summit; it was very beautiful, green, and free of any stones or pebbles. I was sitting on a platform and without saying a word, I was observing (the seventh chakra). It seemed as if I had never seen life before. The scent of God was in the air. I could feel my breath; the caress of the wind on my face was comforting. I could hear the voice of the earth and sky, and this is the seventh sense, a sense that no one has ever talked about, the sense of reaching oneself, God, life, and success. All of this was God's painting. I, who was light-years away from God, was now closer to God than at any point in my life. From God's perspective, I could see the Earth and the people who appeared lost; I felt amused seeing them. If they were here and saw themselves, they would at least be embarrassed by how hastily they were straying off the path. Here, I did not see bad things, or perhaps I did not want to see them. I no longer thought about the base things specific to Earth, such as jealousy, lies, deceit, and trickery. How much it even pains me to be reminded of those base earthly things.

Here, the scent of love comes, the scent of sincerity and help. The scent of good wishes for one another, unexpected kindness, forgiveness, and the scent of God is present...

I have experienced all of this, and it was in that moment that I realized I had not been brought here in vain or by mere chance; everything had been arranged for me. I had been invited to God's party and felt I had the permission to invite guests. I love it so much that I want everyone to see this beautiful frame that I see. I decided to write these down so that they reach everyone, so that all, regardless of language, belief, religion, or any gender or age, come towards the success and life that God has created for them. At this point, I understood the purpose of my life and conveyed that life, despite its chaos, has rules that were written for us years ago, and we remained unaware of them. Life is about knowing oneself, one's

God, understanding love, purpose, and mission. Life is not only not a lie; it is the only truth of which we are unaware. Life is the opportunity provided for us to reach our essence.

By practicing simple exercises, you steer the world towards a positive frequency that brings it closer to its essence and allows us to experience a sense of worthiness (the eighth chakra), and our mission on Earth is nothing more than this.

*"Did I create you in vain?"*

www.ingramcontent.com/pod-product-compliance
Lightning Source LLC
Chambersburg PA
CBHW061959040426
42447CB00010B/1819